OVERWATCH HACKS

OVERWATCH HACKS

THE UNOFFICIAL GAMER'S GUIDE

JASON R. RICH

Sky Pony Press
New York

Copyright © 2018 by Hollan Publishing, Inc.

The Overwatch game is copyright © by Blizzard Entertainment, Inc.

Sky Pony Press books may be purchased in bulk at special discounts for sales promotion, corporate gifts, fund-raising, or educational purposes. Special editions can also be created to specifications. For details, contact the Special Sales Department, Sky Pony Press, 307 West 36th Street, 11th Floor, New York, NY 10018 or info@skyhorsepublishing.com.

Sky Pony® is a registered trademark of Skyhorse Publishing, Inc.®, a Delaware corporation.

Visit our website at www.skyponypress.com.

10 9 8 7 6 5 4 3 2 1

Library of Congress Cataloging-in-Publication Data is available on file.

Cover design by Brian Peterson
Cover image by iStockphoto

Hardcover ISBN: 978-1-5107-4022-8
E-book ISBN: 978-1-5107-4023-5

Printed in the United States of America

TABLE OF CONTENTS

OVERWATCH HACKS

SECTION I:
OVERVIEW OF OVERWATCH

Welcome to a future version of Earth. War has destroyed much of the planet. It's now time for a group of heroes to rebuild and try to make things better. In Overwatch, instead of being a soldier tasked with defeating your enemies single-handedly, in most gameplay modes you are part of a six-person team.

Overwatch has become one of the most popular team-oriented, multi-player shooting games in the world.

Unlike in other first-person shooters, you must work together with your allies to achieve victory in battle, as well as complete specific mission objectives. Once you select a hero and join a team, you're transported to one of numerous locations around the world where the action quickly unfolds.

While Overwatch brings together a ragtag collection of human soldiers, robots, cyborgs, and genetically engineered animals—a.k.a. heroes—who fight together in teams, the game itself doesn't have too much of a storyline. Instead, what transpires in matches depends on the individual characters that make up each team, and the location where the action takes place. However, if you're a noob (a new or low-ranked player), you'll discover that each hero has their own unique backstory, which often reveals how their special powers or capabilities came to be.

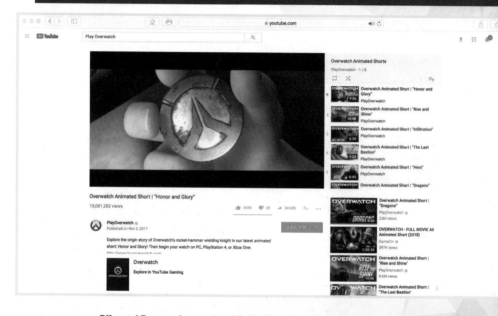

Blizzard Entertainment's official *Play Overwatch* YouTube channel (https://www.youtube.com/user/blizzard) offers a collection of animated videos that reveal relevant plotlines and hero backgrounds not included in the game itself, so be sure to check it out!

Each game map (location) offers a unique layout, a different selection of obstacles, and specific objectives your team must achieve to be victorious. Each hero is unique right from the start, but can be further customized with skins, weapons, victory poses, sprays, voice lines, and highlight intros that can be unlocked by individual players. In fact, each hero has between sixty-eight and ninety-four possible unlocks that can be earned, acquired, or purchased over time.

Lijiang Tower is just one of the exotic destinations you'll soon be visiting.

Overwatch Is Almost Identical Across Hardware Platforms

Currently available for the Playstation 4, Xbox One, and Windows-based PCs, *Overwatch: Game of the Year* is basically the same across all gaming platforms. The biggest difference is the control you have over heroes when playing with the PS4 DualShock 4 controller or Xbox One controller versus a computer keyboard and mouse.

The game requires Internet connectivity, along with a membership to PlayStation Plus (PS4), Xbox Live Gold (Xbox One), or BlizzardBattle.net (PC). You're about to experience a game that, since its release in May 2016, has won more than one hundred "Game of the Year" awards and has more than 35 million active players around the world.

Blizzard Entertainment continues to release regular game updates and patches, which often introduce new heroes and maps, tweak the capabilities of existing heroes, and sometimes add new gameplay modes or elements. So if you notice something different in this guide, chances are it's a result of a new update or patch. This guide is based on the *Overwatch: Game of the Year* edition.

Moira was the 26th hero to be added to the game.

Hero #27 (a Support hero named Brigitte), was released into the game in March 2018. (Visit: https://news.blizzard.com/ en-us/overwatch/21590096/new-hero-first-look-brigitte to learn more.) Brigitte's primary weapon is a Rocket Flail. She also has a Barrier Shields and Shield Dash, along with other powerful moves.

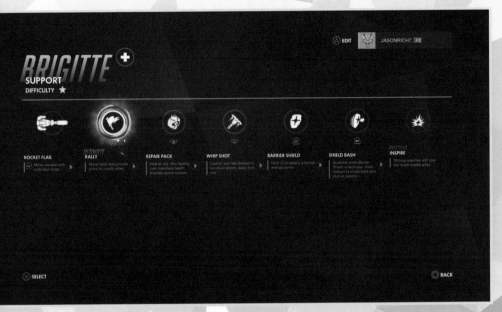

Brigitte's Ultimate move is called Rally. It allows her to move faster, plus provide armor to allies who are close to her.

SECTION II
QUICK TIPS FOR GETTING STARTED

**Soldier: 76 is one of Overwatch's Offense Heroes,
and the first one you'll meet in the Training mode.**

As a noob in the world of Overwatch, begin by mastering the challenges offered in Training mode. Here, starting with Soldier: 76, you'll be introduced to the heroes and the basics for controlling them.

Tracer will guide you through the Tutorial. This is a vital first step to your training.

During a training session, listen to Athena (the computer voice) and follow Tracer throughout the practice areas. Learn the core movement and fighting skills you'll need to master before participating in battles/matches.

Abilities

Main Weapon Details

Health Meter

Ammo Rounds Remaining / Total Ammo Rounds

Just like in the other gameplay modes, as the Tutorial gets under way, your hero's Health Meter is displayed in the lower-left corner of the screen. When this Health Meter is fully depleted, your hero is toast.

Ultimate Ability Icon & Meter

Near the bottom-right corner of the screen, details about your hero's main weapon are displayed. Listed above the weapon is the number of ammo rounds remaining, along with the total number of rounds the weapon can hold. So if the ammo counter says 15/25, you have fifteen out of a maximum of twenty-five rounds remaining.

In almost all cases, when ammo runs out, your hero's main weapon will reload automatically. It's often more convenient, however, for you to manually reload by pressing the [SQUARE] (PS4)/[X] (Xbox One) button. By manually reloading, you can ensure you won't temporarily be without ammo while reloading during a critical moment in battle.

In addition to mastering basic weapon use, Tutorial mode teaches you about a hero's Abilities and Ultimate Abilities, and the cooldown time that's often required in between when each can be used. Your hero's Abilities (and the buttons to utilize them) are displayed to the left of your weapon icon.

From the Main Menu, select Play, then choose between Quick Play, Arcade, Competitive Play (shown), and Game Browser.

Once you reach level 25 as a player, you can engage in Competitive Play mode. By winning these matches, you'll earn points that can be redeemed for a golden version of the main weapon your hero uses.

Wait for your hero's Ultimate Ability to light up after it charges to 100%. It's then ready to use when you decide it could have the most impact.

A hero's Ultimate Ability is their most powerful weapon or tool, but it takes time to charge. The gauge for your hero's Ultimate Ability is displayed near the bottom-center of the screen. Wait until the gauge says 100%, then you can use it by pressing the [TRIANGLE] (PS4)/[Y] (Xbox One) button.

By attacking enemies, your Ultimate Ability meter will recharge faster.

The Ultimate Ability Gauge automatically replenishes over time, but replenishment speed increases when you inflict damage on your enemies using other weapons. If you're controlling a healer, your Ultimate Ability automatically replenishes faster when you heal other team members.

NAVIGATION ICONS

Navigation icons take on different appearances and colors, depending on the map and your situation. Here, the blue diamond represents the object you need to defend (that's off in the distance) and the tiny downward-pointing arrows represent team members.

When it's time to navigate around a map, follow the directional icons that inform you which way to go, and where your teammates, enemies, and objectives can be found.

Early on, practice maneuvering, targeting, and shooting and reloading your weapons, since these are core skills you'll need to be able to handle simultaneously during actual battles or matches.

You may want to complete the Tutorial several times so you become very comfortable moving, aiming, and shooting at the same time. When the Tutorial is complete, stay within Training mode and select the Practice Range or Practice vs. AI mode to continue perfecting your fighting skills before participating in actual battles/matches.

Choose any hero and practice working with them within the Practice Range.

Practice Range allows you to choose any hero, and then practice working with that character in a shooting range environment. You'll encounter Training Bots to use for target practice as you explore this area. Don't get too overconfident, however. These bots are much easier to kill than actual AI- or human-controlled opponents.

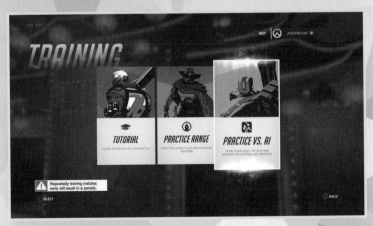

Practice vs. AI mode allows you to select any hero and engage in combat along with equally skilled human team members. Here, you'll fight against computer-controlled opponents. This training mode is ideal for helping you enhance your tactical skills while working with various heroes in actual fighting scenarios.

There's No "I" in Team

After you choose a gameplay mode, a map will be selected for you as a game is found for you to join. Next, choose the hero you want to control.

Overwatch is a team-based game. Your hero selection should be based on your team's overall composition and the map on which you'll be fighting. As challenges for your team evolve, your hero choice will often need to change. A solid, well-rounded team should consist of experts in Offense, Defense, Tank, and Support. A team should contain heroes filling each of these key roles.

From the Assemble Your Team screen in the various Play modes, look for yellow banners that alert you about which hero roles are currently lacking on your team. To increase your chances of victory, fill one of the empty roles. Later, be ready to adapt your hero selection based on the challenges imposed by the enemy team during a match.

Early on, practice working with at least one hero that fills each of the key roles (Offense, Defense, Tank, and Support), so once you identify a weakness in your team, you can quickly choose a hero you're already familiar with, and who fills a vital role that's needed by your team.

Having too many Offense heroes, with no Support or Tank heroes, for example, puts your team at a huge disadvantage. While you may perform well as an individual player during a match, your team has a much higher chance of failure if it's not well balanced with heroes filling all the critical roles.

Know Your Role

Blizzard Entertainment regularly releases updates and additions to Overwatch. This includes the introduction of new heroes. As of early 2018, the game includes twenty-seven unique and powerful heroes, which can be seen in the Hero Gallery. Each hero has a role within the game (Offense, Defense Tank, or Support), as well as a star-based Difficulty level, which indicates a gamer's skill level needed to successfully control the character.

Once you choose a hero and know your role, do your job! Take on the responsibilities of that role and support your teammates. This is how to succeed, as opposed to wandering off on your own.

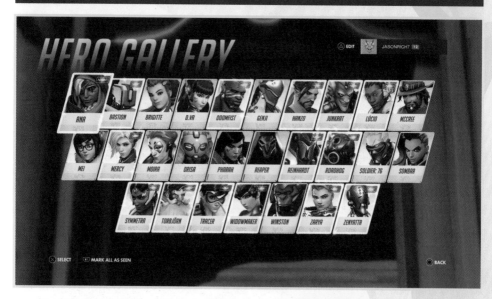

From the Hero Gallery, you can learn about each of the Overwatch heroes, one at a time.

- Offense heroes are the ones capable of inflicting the most damage on opponents. These are the heroes who find, engage, and attack enemies in combat. They move fast and can initiate powerful attacks, but have low defensive capabilities (HP). Doomfist, Genji, McCree, Pharah, Reaper, Soldier: 76, Sombra, and Tracer can fill the Offense role(s) on a team.
- Heroes filling the Defense role are ideal for fortifying locations, protecting other team members, and keeping enemies from advancing. Bastion, Hanzo, Junkrat, Mei, Torbjörn, and Widowmaker are Overwatch's Defense heroes.
- The role of a Tank hero is to break apart groups of enemies and use brute force to enter areas that are heavily fortified by enemy troops. These heroes can withstand direct attacks for the longest amount of time because they have the strongest armor and the most HP. Some of these guys have

special shielding capabilities, making them ideal for drawing enemy fire away from teammates. Your Tank hero options include: D. Va, Orisa, Reinhardt, Roadhog, Winston, and Zarya.

- A team's survival relies heavily on heroes filling the Support role. These characters, including Ana, Brigitte, Lúcio, Mercy, Moira, Symmetra, and Zenyatta, can heal and shield fellow team members, while boosting their ability to inflict damage upon enemies. Support heroes have minimal attack capabilities and low HP, so while other heroes rely on them to stay strong in battle, Support heroes rely on team members for protection, as they can't defend themselves too well.

A team should include heroes that bring different skills to the table.

If your team is lacking a Healer (Ana, Lúcio, Mercy, or Zenyatta, for example), but the opposing team has one, your team is almost guaranteed to lose. This is also the case with Tank heroes. If your team doesn't have one, you could find it very hard or impossible to break through well-guarded enemy areas which are critical to achieving objectives.

You'll discover that certain characters are particularly useful battling against specific other heroes, while others are better at protecting members of your team or for maintaining a stronghold in a specific area.

Teams that really strategize together often assign a sniper to take the high ground as much as possible, so that the hero can shoot enemies from above as a battle transpires on ground level. Unlike other types of heroes, the damage to an enemy that a sniper inflicts does not decrease based on distance.

With their long-range main weapon, Ana, Widowmaker, and Hanzo, for example, can each perform sniper duties.

Because each hero's abilities are unique, from the Assemble Your Team screen, if you plan to add a second hero in a particular role (Offense, Defense, Tank, or Support) to your team, choose a hero that's very different from one your team member already selected.

Moving forward, always pay attention to the choices your opponents make and the challenges you're facing, then adapt your hero selection and strategy as needed. When necessary, change heroes by returning to your team's Spawn Room on a map, and then hold down the [Square] (PS4)/(X) (Xbox One) button.

The Hero Gallery allows you to scroll through the heroes, select one, and:

- Read their backstory
- Learn about their specialty and maneuverability
- Discover details about about their weapon(s), Abilities, and Ultimate Ability
- Customize details relating to a hero's appearance, sounds, and actions using options that must first be unlocked.

From the Hero Gallery, select any hero's photo to view a hero-specific details screen.

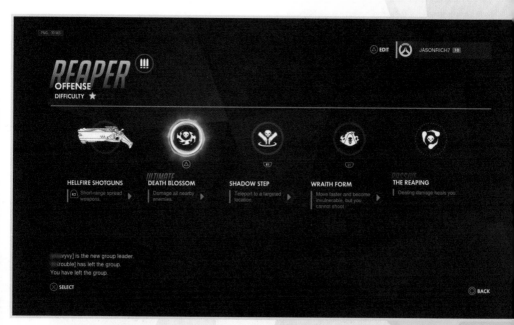

From a hero's overview screen, press the [SQUARE] (PS4)/[X] (Xbox One) button to view details about the hero's weapon(s), Abilities, and Ultimate Ability.

During a battle or match, make a point to regroup with your teammates often. Set an immediate objective and proceed forward as a united front. If multiple team members are defeated at once, make a plan to regroup once everyone respawns.

SECTION III:

INFLICTING DAMAGE IS A KEY TO SUCCESS IN BATTLE

The combined and proficient use of your selected hero's movement capabilities, along with their primary weapon, Abilities, and Ultimate Ability, will be how you're able to contribute to your team's success in battle. Thus, in addition to knowing the impact your weapon(s) will have, precise aim always works to your advantage. For example, a headshot always imposes more damage onto your opponent than a body shot. But with you and your opponent moving around, a headshot is often difficult to achieve.

Aim carefully whenever possible, but when you're being overwhelmed by enemies, just keep shooting in their general direction.

Your hero's main weapon has unlimited ammo. In most cases, you just need to reload periodically. It's nice to take the time needed to line up the perfect headshot, but this is rarely feasible in battles. Do it when you can, but at other times, fire your weapon toward your enemy and keep firing. Chances are you'll cause some damage. At the very least, your Ultimate Ability will recharge faster, giving you the chance to inflict serious damage if you use it at a moment when multiple enemies are nearby.

Tips for Improving Your Aim

Enemies are always outlined in red. This makes them easy to spot, even if they're moving quickly.

**Learning to aim your hero's weapon(s) is an essential skill.
Take full advantage of the Practice Range.**

Use these strategies to help improve your aim:

- **Practice.** Spend a lot of time at the Practice Range, aiming and shooting at Training Bots, both while your hero is standing still and while your hero is moving. Repetition is the key to developing your own muscle memory and improving your reflexes. Because most of the Training Bots don't shoot back, you can focus more on perfecting your moving, aiming, positioning, and shooting skills, as opposed to staying alive in actual battles. The need for repetition and practice in working with a hero can't be emphasized enough!

- **Position Yourself for Clarity.** Make sure you can see the entire game screen clearly. Depending on the size of your monitor, try moving closer or farther away. If you need glasses or contact lenses to improve your vision, wear them when playing Overwatch. A lot of minute detail is displayed on the game screen. If anything looks even slightly blurry, you could miss seeing a critical detail, or have trouble accurately aiming a weapon.

How to Customize the Controls in Advance to Improve Aiming Accuracy

Step #1 - From the main menu, select Options.

Step #2 -Decide whether you want to adjust the settings for All Heroes, or create separate settings for each hero. Advanced gamers often adjust each hero's settings separately.

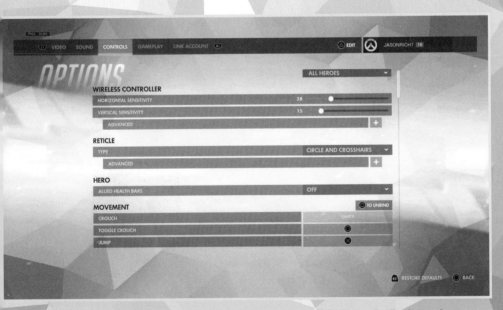

Step #3 -Access the Control menu. On a PS4 or Xbox One, adjust the Horizontal Sensitivity and Vertical Sensitivity, making it easier for you to move your hero and adjust the targeting crosshair (reticle) during high-action sequences. The settings you adjust here should be based on personal preference, not the settings used by more highly skilled gamers. Tinker a bit and see what works best for you, based on your skill level as a gamer.

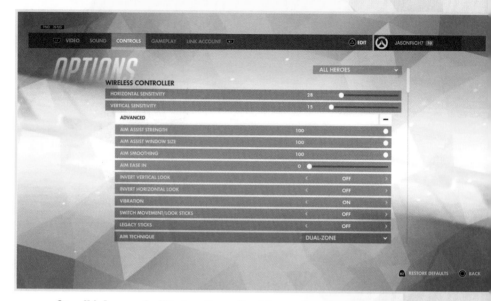

Step #4 -Access the Wireless Controller Advanced menu, and if necessary, increase the options related to aim. For example, based on the hero you typically control, you may opt to make the Aim Assist Window Size larger or smaller.

Step #5 -Access the Reticle menu, and choose the option that you find most appealing, and that stands out to your own eyes on the screen. When you're shooting at an enemy, perfect positioning of the reticle will mean the difference between landing a headshot, making a body shot, or missing completely.

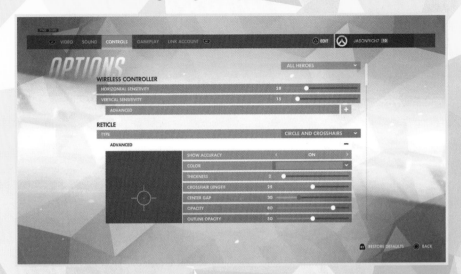

Step #6 - From the Reticle Advanced menu, change the color of the reticle to bright green. This is the color that stands out the most on a busy game screen, so it's easiest to see and position during a battle. Depending on your screen size, consider also increasing the Thickness of the reticle from this menu. You want the size and color of the reticle to be easy to spot, but not so large that it blocks the visible details of your targets.

During a battle, prepare for a shot in advance by pre-adjusting the reticle to the perfect height for your intended target. Wait for your target's head to be directly in line with the reticle, or position the reticle horizontally as needed. When everything is lined up perfectly, start shooting. Depending on your selected hero, the weapon being used, and your distance from the target, you might need to start shooting a fraction of a second in advance. If you have to adjust the height and horizontal position of the reticle at the same time once an enemy becomes visible, you'll waste valuable time, and will often miss ideal shot opportunities.

25

Prepare for Close Combat

Each hero can perform a quick melee attack, which is ideal for close combat, without utilizing a weapon's ammo.

A melee attack is fast, and more accurate than using most weapons at close range. It also typically causes more damage. The drawback is that you need to get in really close to your enemy.

Use a melee attack to finish off an already weakened opponent. If they're still strong but up close, a melee attack will weaken or perhaps momentarily stun an enemy, allowing you to quickly move backward and use your weapon more effectively.

More often than not, a basic attack using a weapon can become more intense when used in conjunction with a hero's specialty movement capabilities, such as short-range teleportation.

When there's not a solid barrier or wall behind you, an enemy can easily sneak up and flank you from behind before you even sense they're nearby. (Flanking means attacking an enemy from any direction except head-on.)

Listen carefully for approaching footsteps. Typically, the enemies with the loudest footsteps and the weapons that make the most noise are the most dangerous. If you crouch when walking, however, your footsteps become much quieter. This makes it easier to sneak up behind an enemy.

SECTION IV:

USE YOUR SURROUNDINGS TO YOUR TACTICAL ADVANTAGE

Almost every map (game location) includes very narrow areas that groups of heroes will need to pass through quickly to reach a specific destination. This makes them temporarily vulnerable to attack. By guarding these chokepoints with appropriate Tank heroes and snipers, for example, it's possible to halt enemies in their tracks or slow them down dramatically in order to prevent them from reaching key objectives.

While working as a team in battle, it sometimes makes sense to assign one Offense hero with a long-range projectile weapon to a position near the opposing team's respawn location. Then, as enemy heroes rejoin the game, a sniper, for example, can easily knock them off from a distance. If done correctly, you can surprise your opponents.

Every map in Overwatch is chock full of places to hide before launching a surprise attack, as well as walls or objects you can stand behind for protection. There are also plenty of places to climb up, so you can look down at your enemies and shoot at them from above.

28

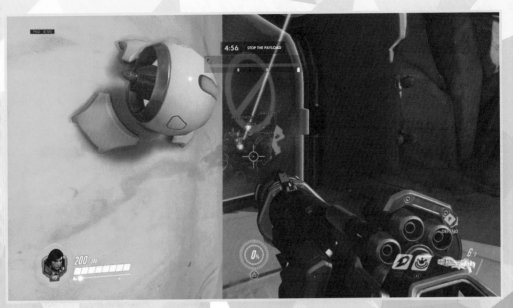

Use solid walls and nearby objects to shield yourself and to help prevent flank attacks. When your side or back is to a solid wall, an enemy can't approach from that side.

Don't just look at the pretty scenery as you're wandering around and exploring each map. Look for ways to use each area and the contents within it to your tactical advantage—either to help you launch an attack, or to help protect yourself and your team.

As your team is escorting a payload, stand to the side or behind the payload and use it as shielding, especially if you're controlling an Offense or Support hero. Staying close to the payload will also boost your hero's HP.

Often you can jump onto a payload and ride it at the same time you're protecting it.
Be ready for attacks from above, as well as from all sides.

Beware of Dangerous Terrain

It's easy to get caught in the crossfire if you're traveling through a chokepoint, but each map is filled with other obstacles that, if you're not careful, can cause major damage or instant death.

You can stand on top of a ledge or cliff and flank an enemy from above,
but don't accidently fall to your death.

If you're walking backwards or running forward without paying attention, don't accidently fall off a cliff. A short drop probably won't hurt you, but a mid-length fall will deplete a lot of HP and falling off a tall ledge or cliff will send you back to the respawn room. If you perish as a result of a fall, this wastes valuable time, as you'll need to wait until your hero respawns and travels back to your previous location from your team's respawn location.

SECTION V:

WORK TOGETHER AS MUCH AS POSSIBLE

Don't forget: In almost every situation when two or more of your teammates are in close proximity and working together, you'll be able to benefit from each other's strengths. For example, a Defense or Tank hero can take incoming fire and create a distraction while an Offense hero launches an attack. Likewise, a Support hero can shadow an Offense hero and replenish their HP as needed to keep him strong, allowing for an extended, more devastating attack.

Maintaining Your Hero's Health

In the Practice Range and in actual battles, you'll come across Health Packs. These are essential to your survival because they replenish your hero's health (HP).

The locations of Health Packs always remain the same on various maps, so knowing where to find them when they're needed will help you keep your hero alive. Once a Health Pack is used, it spawns again (reappears) within a few seconds.

Heroes can be protected simultaneously by shields, armor, and health—displayed as colored layers on the hero's Health Meter. Each character comes with a different combination of shields, armor, and health, which is one thing that makes them unique.

Work Together as Much as Possible

A SMALL HEALTH PACK REPLENISHES 75 HP.

YOU'LL TYPICALLY FIND HEALTH PACKS HIDDEN ON THE FLOOR IN ROOMS WITHIN THE VARIOUS MAPS.

A LARGE HEALTH PACK RESTORES 250 HP TO YOUR HERO'S HEALTH METER.

Each segment on the Health Meter is equal to 25 HP. Shields are displayed on the Health Meter in blue (see the lower-left corner of the screen) and begin to regenerate automatically after not taking damage for at least three seconds. Health Packs and healing from allied heroes also can replenish shields.

Armor is displayed on the Health Meter in yellow (see the lower-left corner of the screen). Armor is most useful against fast-firing weapons but isn't as useful when you're being attacked by larger, single-instance weapons. There are two types of armor: natural and given. Natural armor can be healed but given armor can't be healed during battle.

Once your armor is gone, as your hero receives damage, their Health level will deteriorate. Health is depicted in white on the Health Meter. While Health can be healed with Health Packs or by a Support hero's healing abilities, with few exceptions it does not regenerate on its own.

During incoming attacks, first a hero's shields get depleted, followed by their armor. Only then do attacks diminish a hero's health. When a hero's health is gone, their life ends. So if a Health Pack isn't nearby, quickly seek out healing help from a Support team member to stay alive.

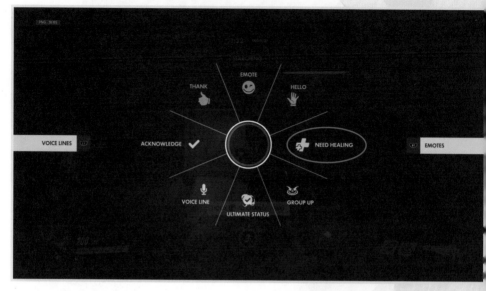

Use the "Need Healing" dialogue command to quickly call for assistance from your team's Support hero(s).

A hero's defeat is not final in Overwatch.

After a pre-defined period, a fallen hero respawns (and returns to their team's starting location on the map). From this location, you can keep your existing hero, or opt to switch heroes as needed. How much time until you respawn is displayed in the top-right corner of the screen.

By learning the layout of the maps in advance when practicing using the Practice vs. AI mode, for example, you'll discover shortcuts for quality navigating back to the action after your hero respawns. Those valuable seconds navigating back to where you're needed can mean the difference between victory and defeat in battles.

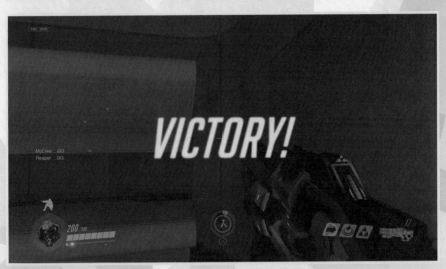

Depending on the gameplay mode selected, a match ends when that map's victory conditions are met by one of the teams.

If you perform well, you could earn the Play of the Game achievement and see a replay of your expert technique.

The Play of the Game is replayed for all to see after each match.
Look for the Play of the Game banner, which also lists the player who won
this award, in the top-left corner of the screen.

After a match, each teammate chooses a player whom they believe was the biggest
asset. The more votes you receive, the bigger your bonus.

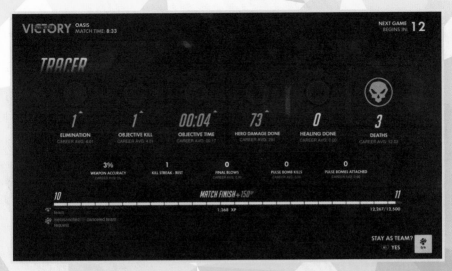

At the conclusion of a match, a series of summary screens show everyone's contributions, as well as your own level progress.

The On-Fire Meter Can Boost Your Ego

Displayed directly below a hero's Health Meter is their On-Fire Meter. As you successfully perform well in the game, this meter moves to the right.

When the blue flame reaches beyond the tiny triangle (see the lower-left corner of the screen), your hero is considered to be "on fire." This means you're doing very well during the current battle or match.

Upon achieving the on-fire status, your profile photo next to your Health Meter gets framed with a blue flame. As a gamer, you're now a threat to be reckoned with. While this gives you bragging rights and may cause opponents to get nervous, achieving the "on fire" status does not enhance the strength, HP, or any attributes of your hero.

When you see a tiny flame icon accompanied by a number appear on the screen after defeating an enemy or accomplishing a task, this means your On-Fire Meter has been given a boost by the amount indicated by the number.

Stay Together in Battle

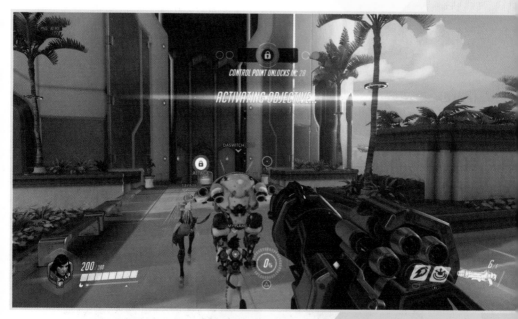

If you're unsure of the terrain, and you're not yet fully comfortable controlling the hero you've selected, stick with your teammates as you explore the map during a match.

Sure, you can also follow the navigational icons that pop up on the screen to help you find your way, but if you follow other allied heroes who know where they're going, you won't get lost, and you can easily protect each other.

By allowing one or more Defense heroes to lead the way as you move forward as a group, the Offense, Tank, and Support heroes can take advantage of a Defense hero's shielding capabilities. This offers added protection in case you accidently walk into an ambush or surprise attack.

SECTION VI:
WHAT TO DO WHILE WAITING TO RESPAWN

Even if you become a pro, your hero is going to perish—often several times—during each match.

After your hero's demise, a countdown clock appears in the top-right corner of the screen telling you how much time until your character respawns and you can return to battle.

Depending on the reason for your most recent death and the number of times you've been defeated during the current battle or match, the time to respawn will vary. Use this time wisely!

First, don't get angry and allow your emotions to cloud your judgment. Don't pout! Use the downtime to strategize! Closely watch your teammates in action as the battle ensues. This is called Death Watching. Quickly view the action from each team member's point of view and figure out where everyone is and what challenges they're currently facing. Press R2 or L2 (PS4)/LT or RT (Xbox One) to switch between hero POVs while Death Watching.

When re-visiting the Spawn Room after you've been temporarily defeated, you have the option to select a different hero to control. Make your decision quickly. As soon as the respawn period ends, you can return to battle, and you don't want to waste a second being idle.

Five Ways to Stay Busy While Waiting to Respawn

While waiting to respawn, plan your next attacks and strategies. Things to consider include:

- Do you want to keep your current hero, or switch heroes based on how the battle is playing out?
- Once you respawn, to what location do you want to return? What's the quickest way to get there?
- Have other team members been killed at the same time? Can you travel together as a group back to the previous fighting location while protecting each other along the way?
- If returning to a previous fighting location, what do you need to do differently to stay alive? If traveling to a new location, what fighting strategies will you adopt right away?
- Consider talking to your teammates during your downtime. Figure out who might need immediate help when you return to the game or plan your next mega-attack. Before you know it, you'll be back in the action!

SECTION VII:
CUSTOMIZE YOUR FAVORITE HEROES

By winning battles and performing well, you'll gain levels as a player.

Each time you increase a level, you receive one Loot Box that contains the ability to customize your favorite heroes from within the Hero Gallery. Similar customization options can also be purchased within Loot Boxes. Each Loot Box is filled with a random selection of customization options.

Select the Loot Box option from the main menu, then hold down the [X] (PS4)/[A] Xbox One button to open a box you already have.

Press the [SQUARE] (PS4)/[X] (Xbox One) button to use real money to purchase 2 ($1.99), 5 ($4.99), 11 ($9.99), 24 ($19.99), or 50 ($39.99) Loot Boxes from the Shop. Cosmetic rewards, such as hero skins, change a character's appearance but do not affect their gameplay abilities.

Once you earn or purchase one or more Loot Boxes, it's time to open them one at a time.

Each Loot Box contains a random selection of items you can use to customize specific heroes. Select and choose one item at a time to Preview it, and then Equip it (link it with a hero you'll control).

If you receive this Voice Line for Winston, for example, and you Equip Winston with it during a match, you'll be able to make Winston say the newly acquired line.

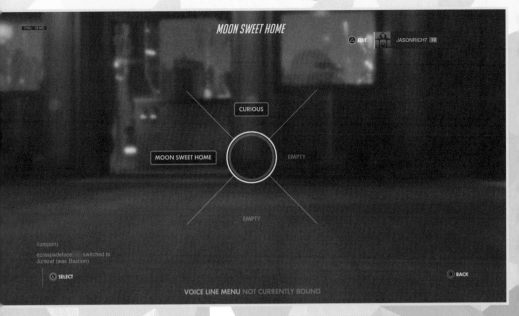

When you acquire a Voice Line, assign it a location on the Voice Line menu, so you can access and use it anytime moving forward. Once you acquire an item from a Loot Box, such as a Voice Line or Character Skin, it's yours to keep forever.

Acquiring a skin from a Loot Box allows you to alter a hero's appearance, not their strength or capabilities. Shown here is Tracer's Neon Green skin.

Once you Equip it, you can alter Tracer's appearance after selecting her before a match, then highlighting and selecting the Select Skin option located in the top-right corner of the screen. From the pull-down menu, choose from the available skins. The Neon Green option is selected here.

Here, Tracer's Slipstream skin is selected.
As you can see, swapping skins gives your hero an instant makeover.

Kick Start Your Overwatch Career

Every time you accomplish something impressive within Overwatch, you'll unlock a commemorative badge of honor.

Awards won during matches, along with an overview of your other achievements, trophies, experience level, and play style, can be seen by accessing the Career Profile option from the main menu.

It's the information collected as part of your Career Profile that determines how you get paired up with random human- or AI-controlled opponents, based on which gameplay mode you select. Over time, the game tracks a player's successes based on a variety of criteria beyond just wins and losses. For example, how well a player utilizes their hero's unique powers and abilities is measured, ranked, and tracked.

SECTION VIII:
CHOOSE A GAME MODE TO MATCH YOUR STATE OF MIND

Depending on the types of challenges you're in the mood for, you'll discover many ways to experience Overwatch based on which game mode you select.

Choose the Play or Training option from the main menu.

If you select the Play gameplay mode, next choose between Quick Play, Arcade, Competitive Play, or Game Browser.

After you select a gameplay mode, a map (playing location) is randomly selected for you. As you'll discover, each map offers a different set of challenges and objectives for the battle or match. Once you know on which map you'll be playing, you and your team then each select a hero to control.

Overwatch's GamePlay Modes

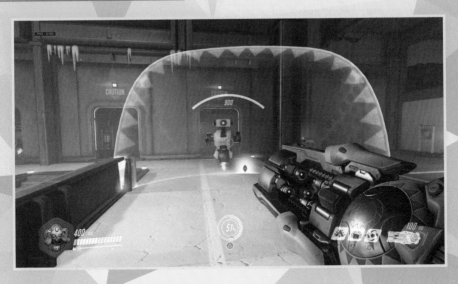

The popular gameplay modes include:

- **Practice Range:** Select a hero, then learn to work with that character as you battle against Practice Bots. This is a one-player, non-team-oriented gameplay mode that's ideal for getting to know the various heroes and what each is capable of.

- **Play/Practice vs. AI:** This mode allows you to team up with similarly skilled human opponents to make up a team, but you'll battle against computer-controlled adversaries within randomly selected maps. Choose between Easy, Medium, or Hard.
- **Quick Play:** Experience games against other human players typically ranked at a similar skill level as you. This is likely the gameplay mode you'll experience the most. Once in a while, the game will put you up against players at a much higher level than you. However, if you abandon games too often, you will be penalized, so even if you are not evenly matched, do your best.

- **Arcade:** Participate in experimental matches with special rules and unique maps. From this menu, choose between several different types of challenges.
- **Competitive Play:** Once you reach level 25 or higher, you'll complete against other human players, and as you achieve additional victories, you'll be invited to engage in tougher battles against more highly skilled players.

Each Location (Map) Offers Unique Challenges

Based on which gameplay mode you select, a compatible map will be selected for you. Each of the game's 22 maps offers different gameplay elements. There are eight types of maps:

- **Arena:** Here, it's a 1v1 or 3v3 battle with the goal of eliminating all opponents. Maps include: Black Forest, Castillo, Ecopoint: Antarctica, and Necropolis.
- **Assault:** During a pre-set time period, Attackers try to capture various objectives while Defenders attempt to stop them. Maps include: Horizon Lunar Colony, Hanamura, Temple of Anubis, and Volskaya Industries.

- **Assault/Escort:** Attackers must locate and acquire a payload, then safely bring it to a predefined destination, while the defenders attempt to stop the Attackers in their tracks. Maps include: Blizzard World, Eichenwalde, Hollywood, King's Row, and Numbani.
- **Capture the Flag:** Each team of six players must defend its own flag while attempting to acquire the opposing team's flag using brute force and strategy. Maps include: Ilios, Lijiang Tower, Nepal, and Oasis.

Capture the Flag requires members of your team to guard your own flag while other team members seek out and capture the enemy's flag. The first team to successfully capture the opponent's flag and return it to their home area three times wins the match.

- **Control:** Teams battle each other to achieve one pre-defined objective at a time. The first team to successfully complete two objectives wins the match. Maps include: Ilios, Lijiang Tower, Nepal, and Oasis.
- **Deathmatch:** During an eight-player match, players attempt to score the most individual hero defeats possible. Maps include: Chateau Guillard

- **Escort:** Within a pre-set time limit, Attackers attempt to move a payload to a specified delivery location while the Defenders try to keep the Attackers from succeeding. Maps include: Dorado, Junkertown, Route 66, and Watchpoint: Gibraltar.

If your team is assigned to escort a payload, you must ensure it arrives safely to its destination while the enemy team attempts to take control of it.

- **Team Deathmatch**: In a 4v4 match, each team's objective is to defeat the most opponents. Maps include: Ilios, Lijiang Tower, Nepal, and Oasis.

When forming teams, you can play with friends, random human players, or AI-controlled heroes. As you're playing with friends, for example, you're able to chat or talk amongst yourselves. What individual heroes within the game say is based upon Voice Lines that are unlocked over time by players.

Practice Your Fighting Skills, Without Being Able to Level Up

Instead of practicing your skills in conjunction with other human players, from the Play mode, select the Game Browser option.

Step #1: From the Find Game screen, select the Create Game option.

Step #2: From the Create Game screen, select the Add AI option, and insert computer-controlled heroes into all of the empty slots on your team, as well as on team two.

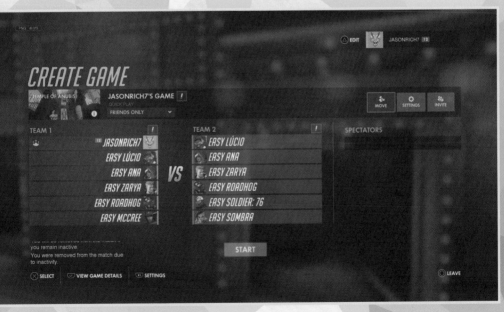

ADD AI

HERO
RECOMMENDED

DIFFICULTY
EASY

EASY
MEDIUM
HARD

BOTH

BACK   ADD

Step #3: When prompted, choose a level of difficulty. If you're first learning how to control the various heroes, choose Easy. However, if you want a more difficult challenge, choose from the Medium or Hard options.

CREATE GAME

TEMPLE OF ANUBIS   JASONRICH7'S GAME
QUICK PLAY
FRIENDS ONLY

MOVE   SETTINGS   INVITE

EDIT   JASONRICH7 12

TEAM 1   TEAM 2   SPECTATORS
JASONRICH7   EASY LÚCIO
EASY LÚCIO   EASY ANA
EASY ANA   VS   EASY ZARYA
EASY ZARYA   EASY ROADHOG
EASY ROADHOG   EASY SOLDIER: 76
EASY MCCREE   EASY SOMBRA

you remain inactive.
You were removed from the match due
to inactivity.

START

SELECT   VIEW GAME DETAILS   SETTINGS   LEAVE

Step #4: Once the Create Game screen has been filled in with AI-controlled heroes and yourself, select the Start option.

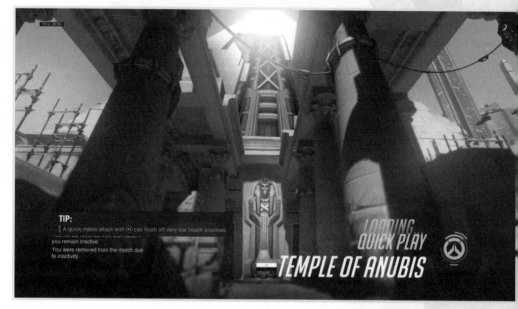

Step #5: You'll be transported to the location displayed in the top-left corner of the Create Game screen.

Step #6: Choose the hero you want to control.

Step #7: The game you create will begin. However, it'll be you teamed up with computer-controlled teammates, being challenged by a team of computer-controlled enemies. This is a great way to brush up on your skills, explore maps, and develop fighting techniques with your favorite heroes, but you won't level up as a player based on your successes.

The Create Game mode can also be used to set up games in which you compete with or against your online friends and/or other human- and AI-controlled heroes.

SECTION IX:

GET TO KNOW OVERWATCH'S HEROES

The ways each hero moves, along with their primary weapon, Abilities, and Ultimate Abilities, are as diverse as their appearances and individual backstories. Some heroes are better at ground level, while others have the ability to hover, fly, teleport, or become invisible as they move.

Becoming a skilled Overwatch player requires you to learn what sets each hero apart so you can make full use of their unique skills when controlling any one of them.

Equally important after choosing the hero you'll control is knowing how to counteract the fighting skills and weapons of whichever heroes you're face to face with at any given moment.

By knowing the capabilities of your adversaries, you can often predict how they'll use their weapon, Ability, and/or Ultimate Ability. Thus, it's often possible to avoid intense attacks, or at least defend yourself and counteract in an appropriate and more impactful way.

Once you get to know Overwatch's heroes, you'll be ready to visit any map and use your chosen hero to defeat enemies, protect your team's flag, transport and defend payloads, or handle whatever other objectives your team is faced with. Be sure to invest some time in training, however, to become familiar with the terrain and layout of each map.

Access Overwatch's main menu and select the Hero Gallery option, then highlight and select a hero you want to learn more about. If a hero's profile photo is surrounded by a yellow frame, and a "New" icon is displayed, this means that new customizable options are available that have been unlocked from Loot Boxes.

From a hero's profile screen, press the [Square](PS4)/[X] (Xbox One) button to reveal the Hero Info screen. From here, discover the game controller button presses needed to use each hero's weapon(s), Abilities, and Ultimate Ability.

Keep in mind that when you see Hero Info screens throughout this guide, it's for the PS4 version of Overwatch. While the weapon(s), Abilities, and Ultimate Abilities are the same for each hero in all versions of the game, the controller or keyboard/mouse buttons you need to use are different for the Xbox One and PC versions of Overwatch.

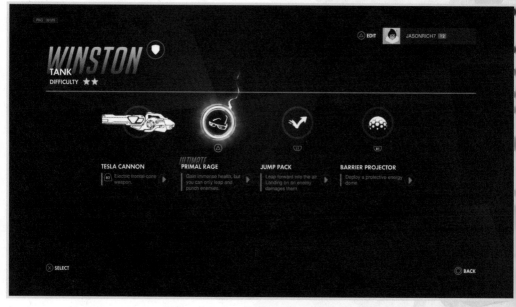

Highlight the circular (blue) right-pointing arrow icon associated with a weapon, Ability, or Ultimate Ability, then press the [X] (PS4)/[A] (Xbox One) button to see an animated demonstration.

The Defense Heroes

To get to know the various Defense Heroes, choose a favorite, then practice working with that hero.

Bastion

Difficulty	Main Weapon	Ability #1	Ability #2	Ultimate Ability
*	**Sentry** or **Recon Configuration** Serves either as a stationary rotary cannon (sentry configuration) or as an automatic weapon while on-the-go (recon configuration). Reconfigure it on command and as needed.	**Self Repair** Has the ability to heal himself.	**Ironclad** Receives less damage from incoming attacks.	**Tank Configuration** Can transform into a mobile tank with a powerful cannon, giving you massive fighting power on the go!

This guy is a damage dealer with a high "DPS" (damage per second) ranking. Because he's a self-healer, he does not rely on a Support hero or Health Packs to stay strong in battle.

He can turn his gun 360 degrees, as well as up and down, when he's serving as a stationary Sentry. However, Bastion can't move forward or backward. This makes him an easy target, unless he's protected by team members.

Bastion's weapons work better in the short- to mid-range but lose accuracy as targets get farther away.

It's not possible for Bastion to land head shots while in Sentry mode. To achieve the most damage, aim for the center of your enemy. When in Recon mode, take the time when possible to aim at your adversary's head.

Hanzo Shimada

Difficulty	Main Weapon	Ability #1	Ability #2	Ultimate Ability
***	**Storm Bow** This mighty bow and arrow is a highly precise long-range weapon. It allows Hanzo to also serve as a sniper.	**Scatter Arrow** One arrow is launched, but upon impact, it splits into several powerful projectiles.	**Sonic Arrow** Temporarily discover the location of hidden enemies when you launch this arrow in a particular direction.	**Dragonstrike** Release a legendary dragon spirit that causes the instant demise of any enemy it passes through.

Hanzo has the ability to jump onto walls to climb them. This makes it fast and often easy for him to reach high areas to serve as a sniper. To climb, face a wall and hold down the Jump button.

The team with one or more snipers that control the highest areas on a map tends to be more successful. Attacking from above makes it easier to achieve head shots against your enemies, while making it harder for them to successfully target a head shot against you from below.

When controlling a character like Hanzo, who can climb up walls to reach higher-up areas, the trick is to find the spots that offer a bird's eye view of strategic map areas. How to reach these areas isn't always obvious. Take the time during training to really explore the maps. Having a sniper positioned above can be useful for many types of team-oriented offensive and defensive strategies.

Hanzo is an expert marksman, meaning he has really accurate aim capabilities with his weapons. But it requires extra practice to control Hanzo like a pro. Use his precision aim to your advantage. Go for head shots whenever possible to inflict the most damage.

Junkrat

Difficulty	Main Weapon	Ability #1	Ability #2	Ultimate Ability
**	**Frag Launcher** This is a projectile weapon that shoots bouncing explosives.	**Concussion Mine** Use Junkrat's strong arm to toss a mine, then detonate it on your command.	**Steel Trap** Toss and place a strong steel trap, and watch enemies flounder around for a bit while trying to escape. Use this to slow down adversaries.	**Rip-Tire** Remotely drive a spiked tire and steer it directly into your enemies to cause more pain (and skid marks).

Junkrat has the unique ability to drop bombs at the moment of his own demise, which will inflict some last-minute harm to the hero who's bested him. This move is called Total Mayhem.

Heroes like Junkrat are great for breaking down enemy shields and barriers, as well as defeating enemy Tanks.

When moving forward in a group, Junkrat can create explosions to help clear the path ahead or push back the enemy. He can also utilize his Steel Trap (shown here) to slow down anyone approaching.

Junkrat is better suited for battle when he's close or mid-range from his adversaries. He's not a good match against heroes targeting him with long-range weapons. Use his Rip-Tire (shown) to plow down enemies in their tracks, but don't forget to steer the tire into your enemies once it's launched.

Mei

Difficulty	Main Weapon	Ability #1	Ability #2	Ultimate Ability
**	**Endothermic Blaster** Use as a short-range weapon that freezes opponents (if held in the freezing beam long enough). This weapon is also able to shoot long-range icicles that will decrease an enemy's HP.	**Cryo-Freeze** While healing yourself, temporarily prevent enemies from causing you further harm as they attack.	**Ice Wall** Create a solid ice wall in front of you that serves as a temporary shield for you and your teammates. It can also serve as a barrier in the enemy's path.	**Blizzard** Control a unique weather drone capable of freezing enemies in their tracks.

Mei is an excellent short-range fighter. She will often last longer in battle than some other heroes because she can heal herself. While she can shoot icicles a decent distance, these are harder to aim accurately.

She may not be cold-hearted, but she can certainly give her enemies a chill. A Long-Range Icicle shot to the head will usually do the trick.

Freezing an enemy typically won't finish them off. Whenever possible, follow up immediately with an icicle to the head to end your opponent.

Before creating an ice wall, pay attention to the locations of your teammates. Make sure you won't accidently block them in an area that leaves them vulnerable to attack. Use ice walls to separate enemies, especially in and around chokepoints. Ice walls should also be used to create temporary chokepoints that work to your team's advantage.

Torbjörn Lindholm

Difficulty	Main Weapon	Ability #1	Ability #2	Ultimate Ability
**	**Rivet Gun** and **Forge Hammer** The Rivet Gun is used as a long-range weapon, but it has a slow firing time. It's also a powerful short-range weapon, but it's not too accurate when it comes to aiming. Use the Forge Hammer to smack turrets and increase their level, or to whack an enemy and inflict damage.	**Armor Pack** Toss this object ahead of you so one of your teammates can grab it and receive additional armor for added protection against enemy attacks.	**Build Turret** At any map location, build a stationary turret that can be upgraded. The turret has a long range. It offers precise aiming capabilities.	**Molten Core** For a short time, Torbjörn can increase the strength of his weapon attacks, enhance his own armor, plus boost a level 2 turret to level 3.

Use the Armor Packs generously to increase the defensive strength of your teammates against attacks.

Any time your team is trying to defend something, Torbjörn can become a great asset.

As Torbjörn is wandering around any map after defeating enemies, collect scraps to gain resources. A separate resource meter is displayed on the screen for this hero.

Practice using Torbjörn's weapons. They can be very powerful, but often pose a challenge to noobs. This hero is best used for defense. When you use Torbjörn's stationary weapons, don't keep positioning them at the same locations on a map or your adversaries will easily determine where they are and be prepared to destroy them.

Widowmaker

Difficulty	Main Weapon	Ability #1	Ability #2	Ultimate Ability
**	**Widow's Kiss** This weapon can be used as a long-range sniper weapon or as an automatic assault rifle for mid-range (or even close-up) attacks.	**Grappling Hook** Launch this hook onto a ledge and quickly pull yourself up. It's a great way to reach high-up areas quickly.	**Venom Mine** From your left hand, launch a poisonous weapon that'll cause a decent level of damage over a several-second period. While the poison is working, use your Widow's Kiss weapon to speed up and intensify the damage you inflict.	**Infra-Sight** You and your teammates will be able to see behind walls and barriers, and temporarily determine exactly where all your enemies are hiding.

The ability to temporarily see behind walls and barriers allows you and your teammates to launch surprise attacks or set up better defenses.

Thanks to Widowmaker's incredible aim, she's very good at knocking off opponents from a long distance with great precision. She's able to defeat most heroes with a single head shot.

Widowmaker's greatest strength is as a sniper. Her poison, however, is not too potent.
She's better when positioned high up so she can pick off opponents from above.

Venom Mine allows Widowmaker to release poison from her left hand.

The Offense Heroes

Meet Overwatch's Offense heroes and discover what makes each of them special.

Doomfist

Difficulty	Main Weapon	Ability #1	Ability #2	Ultimate Ability
***	Hand Cannon An automatically reloading short-range weapon that spreads out its ammo with each shot.	Seismic Slam Smash the ground after taking a leap forward to knock opponents off their feet and cause damage.	Rising Uppercut or Rocket Punch This mighty uppercut punch can catapult an adversary high into the air. The Rocket Punch can be charged up and used head-on against an opponent, who will be thrown backwards.	Meteor Strike Jump high into the air, target your landing spot, and come smashing down to the ground to pummel nearby enemies.

When using a Rocket Punch, if the adversary smashes backwards into a solid wall, their damage increases.

At the same time Doomfist uses his abilities to cause pain and damage on his opponents, he automatically gets surrounded temporarily with a personal shield for protection.

The Hand Cannon can be a useful weapon at mid-range,
but Doomfist's punches are great for close combat.

Use a Meteor Strike to pummel one or more opponents at once.

Genji

Difficulty	Main Weapon	Ability #1	Ability #2	Ultimate Ability
***	Shuriken	Deflect	Swift Strike	Dragonblade
	Simultaneously throw three projectile weapons (throwing stars). Line them up to hit the same target or throw them in an arc to cause less damage but cover a broader target area.	Use this skill to block incoming projectile weapons and deflect them toward whatever direction you're aiming at. When in close range, use it to block a melee attack.	Quickly run forward to launch a close-range attack.	Use a sword-like weapon to launch a power-packed attack at close range.

Genji has the ability to climb up walls and double jump, allowing him to quickly reach areas that are difficult for most other heroes to get to.

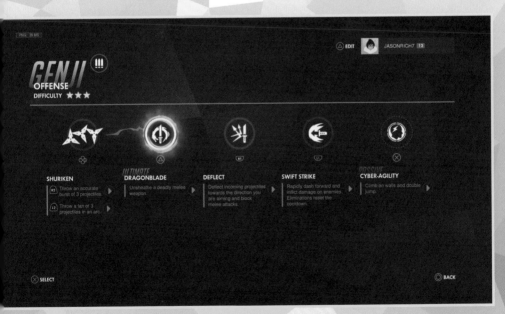

Genji can inflict a lot of damage fast, either when approaching an enemy head-on, or while flanking an adversary. He's also great at finishing off already weakened enemies, which means he works well with teammates.

Genji is one of the most versatile heroes in the game when it comes to mobility. Use this to your advantage. It takes a lot of extra practice to master his skills, so be prepared to put in the necessary training time.

When the time is right and the enemies are relatively close, whip out the Dragonblade and cause mega-damage.

Jesse McCree (known simply as "McCree")

Difficulty	Main Weapon	Ability #1	Ability #2	Ultimate Ability
**	**Peacekeeper** This revolver (handgun) offers two ways to shoot. Aim accurately at your enemies, or fire all remaining rounds in a more haphazard way when there's no time to aim.	**Combat Roll** While reloading your weapon, roll in the direction you're already traveling. This momentarily makes you harder to target.	**Flashbang** Throw this weapon to stun any enemies in front of you. This impact does not last too long, so be prepared to follow up immediately with a weapon attack.	**Dreadeye** A fancy way of shooting that inflicts extra damage on your enemies.

With practice, McCree's weapons can be aimed accurately and cause a high level of damage per second.

Use the Flashbang to enter tight areas and surprise enemies. Just make sure you're able to follow up with immediate attacks from your other weapons, or the stun effect the Flashbang has won't be too useful. This is a great Ability if one or two teammates are nearby and ready to attack the stunned enemy as well.

McCree's greatest weakness is his lack of speed. If he can't fight his way out of a situation, he probably won't be able to retreat fast enough to survive.

If you run out of ammo, use a Combat Roll to escape from a tight spot without the risk of getting shot. Be prepared to resume fighting and shooting as soon as the Combat Roll is complete. If you stand mid-distance from enemies and locate yourself in an enclosed area, you have more time to target each enemy and pick them off one at a time.

Pharah

Difficulty	Main Weapon	Ability #1	Ability #2	Ultimate Ability
*	**Rocket Launcher** This is a long-range projectile weapon that uses exploding ammo. While Pharah can be a sniper, this weapon works equally well at mid-range.	**Jump Jet** Fly directly upwards and hover, or use this move to jump up and propel forward.	**Concussive Blast** From her left arm, this weapon is launched and used to temporarily push back enemies.	**Barrage** Launch a group of mini-rockets at your opponents. They'll cause more damage than the Rocket Launcher's main ammo.

Pharah can continue shooting and using her other weapons while flying or hovering.

Use Pharah's jumping ability to get past difficult environmental obstacles.

The Rocket Launcher is a powerful weapon when used from any distance. Its precision and strength do not diminish when it's launched from a distance.

Wait for Pharah's Barrage to fully charge, then launch a power-packed attack against your enemies.

Reaper

Difficulty	Main Weapon	Ability #1	Ability #2	Ultimate Ability
*	**Hellfire Shotguns** Held in each hand, these are two powerful short-range weapons. Ammo spreads outwards as it's fired alternatively between the two guns.	**Shadow Step** Reaper has the ability to disappear and teleport to another nearby location that you select. This is great for launching surprise attacks and flanking opponents.	**Wraith Form** Although you can't shoot while in this form, you can move quickly without being harmed by your enemies.	**Death Blossom** Inflict damage to all nearby enemies with a single HP diminishing attack.

Any time Reaper inflicts damage on his enemies, he simultaneously heals himself, plus recharges his Death Blossom Ultimate Ability.

Reaper is awesome at close-range fighting. Move in as quickly and as closely as you can to your enemy when launching attacks.

Use the Shadow Step to flank opponents and create an element of surprise. The screen takes on a purple color when Reaper can't be seen.

Both of Reaper's Hellfire guns target the same enemy simultaneously.

Soldier: 76

Difficulty	Main Weapon	Ability #1	Ability #2	Ultimate Ability
*	**Heavy Pulse Rifle** This is a versatile and powerful automatic assault weapon that works well from any distance.	**Sprint** Run faster in a forward direction.	**Helix Rockets** Launch a group of exploding rockets directly at one or more enemies to cause some quick and serious damage.	**Tactical Visor** Use this ability to temporarily auto-aim your weapon at any target that can be seen.

Solider: 76 has the ability to create a temporary Biotic Field that will heal himself and any teammates nearby. When the field is active, a yellow circle appears on the screen. Teammates who want or need to be healed must be within this circle for a few seconds.

Take advantage of the Heavy Pulse Rifle to inflict of lot of DPS (damage per second) on your enemy.

The Sprint Ability will get you where you need to be fast. Just be prepared to attack or defend yourself (and your teammates) once you get there. The Heavy Pulse Rifle will devastate enemies from any distance.

The Helix Rockets can pack a wallop, but they have a long cooldown period. Use them sparingly so they're available when you really need them. The Tactical Visor is turned on here.

Attention Noobs: Soldier: 76 is one of the easiest heroes to control. If you're first learning to play Overwatch, choose this hero often so you can level up faster and focus on mastering other aspects of the game.

Sombra

Difficulty	Main Weapon	Ability #1	Ability #2	Ultimate Ability
***	**Machine Pistol**	**Translocator**	**Stealth**	**EMP**
	This is a short-range automatic weapon that really packs a punch.	Toss a special beacon anywhere in the area, then teleport to that beacon on your command.	Become totally invisible for a limited time and travel around any map freely.	Using an electromagnetic pulse, Sombra can instantly destroy enemy shields or barriers, and simultaneously prevent enemies from using their Abilities or Ultimate Abilities for a short period of time.

Sombra has the ability to see injured enemies through solid walls.

As a technology whiz, Sombra has the ability to literally hack her enemies, so they temporarily can't use their own abilities. She can also hack Health Packs so they respawn faster for her and her teammates (but not for enemies). If Sombra is taking damage from an incoming attack, this slows down her hacking ability.

While your teammates are engaged in a head-on, frontal assault against one or more enemies, Sombra can turn invisible and flank adversaries from the side or behind using her Machine Pistol. Get into the habit of attacking from different directions, so your adversaries never know what to expect. Here, she's tossing her Translocator with her left hand.

Thanks to her ability to teleport, Sombra can get in and out of difficult-to-reach places safely, even when enemies are present. Meanwhile, her ability to hack Health Packs can give your team a huge advantage. Her Machine Pistol (shown) is the perfect go-to weapon as she's exploring maps and working to achieve objectives.

Tracer

Difficulty	Main Weapon	Ability #1	Ability #2	Ultimate Ability
**	**Pulse Pistols**	**Blink**	**Recall**	**Pulse Bomb**
	Cause some damage to your enemies with this matching pair of short-range weapons that fire simultaneously.	Instead of walking, instantly teleport forward in that same direction.	Instantly take a trip back in time to a previous map location and regain whatever health you had there. Use this to compensate for minor mistakes in judgment. You get a second chance at launching successful attacks.	From your hand, emit a powerful burst weapon that explodes on contact.

Tracer is one of the heroes who can easily hunt down her enemies, then sneak up on them from behind to launch an attack. When Tracer is fighting in conjunction with several teammates, have her focus on the opposing team's healer, so enemies who perish will need to take time out of the battle to respawn.

Take advantage of Tracer when your team requires speed and a high DPS to wreak havoc on enemies.

Use her Blink ability to teleport next to or behind an enemy to flank them by surprise.

Tracer doesn't have a lot of HP, so don't leave her exposed and vulnerable for too long. She's much better at taking an approach of move in quickly, attack, then immediately move out.

The Tank Heroes

Get to know Overwatch's mighty Tank heroes.

D. Va

Difficulty	Main Weapon	Ability #1	Ability #2	Ability #3	Ultimate Ability
**	Fusion Cannons A short-range automatic weapon that sprays its ammo to cover a wider range.	Boosters Has the ability to fly in whatever direction this hero is pointed.	Defense Matrix Block against incoming projectile weapons approaching from ahead.	Micro Missiles Launch a group of missiles at the same time.	Self-Destruct or Call Mech After ejecting from her mech, she can make it explode (after a short delay) and use it as a weapon. She's then able to call upon a replacement mech.

When D. Va's mech is destroyed, she can eject out of it and continue fighting, although she'll be a lot weaker. Summon a new mech quickly!

Tank heroes like D. Va or Winston should stay in the front of the pack when a team is progressing forward together.

D. Va's abilities work extra well when she's used in conjunction with another Tank hero. She's best utilized when your team is grouped together and you need to inflict short-range damage. Shown here is the view from her Mech.

Check out D. Va's Peace pose. It's one of several you can unlock from a Loot Box.

Orisa

Difficulty	Main Weapon	Ability #1	Ability #2	Ultimate Ability
**	**Fusion Driver** This is a powerful and automatic projectile weapon. Its main drawback is that while firing, Orisa moves slower.	**Protective Barrier** Toss a high-tech device in front of you, and instantly create a shield that'll protect you and your teammates.	**Fortify** Activate this mega-powerful armor that allows you to become temporarily unstoppable while reducing the amount of damage received by incoming attacks.	**Supercharger** Activate this device to temporarily increase the damage caused by your teammates' attacks against your enemies. (Both teammates and enemies must be nearby.)

Use Orisa's Halt! Ability to toss a grenade-like object at opponents that lures them together and temporarily slows them down.

When your team needs protection using shields, Orisa should be your go-to hero! Just don't allow enemies to get too close to her as she's vulnerable at close range.

Unlike the shields created by some other heroes, keep in mind the ones created by Orisa are strong but stationary. Place them strategically so they offer you and your team the maximum amount of protection. For example, if there's a solid wall behind you and a Protective Barrier in front, it makes it much harder for enemies to successfully attack.

The Fusion Driver can be used to pummel enemies from almost any distance, as long as they can be seen.

Reinhardt Wilhelm

Difficulty	Main Weapon	Ability #1	Ability #2	Ultimate Ability
*	**Rocket Hammer** Use this hammer to initiate devastating melee (close range) attacks.	**Charge** Quickly blast your way forward, crash into an enemy, and smash 'em into a wall to inflict some serious harm.	**Fire Strike** From a distance, launch a projectile energy weapon from your hammer.	**Earthshatter** All enemies in front of Reinhardt get thrown to the ground when this Ultimate Ability is used. It typically depletes all of an enemy's remaining HP instantly.

Reinhardt can protect himself and his teammates by creating a Barrier Field in front of him. This is a strong energy shield that offers top-notch protection for everyone behind it. The shield moves forward as Reinhardt moves forward, making it ideal for advancing safely while launching attacks. He's typically a great addition to any well-rounded team that's taking an offensive posture in battle.

Use the Charge maneuver to run forward and smash an enemy against a wall.

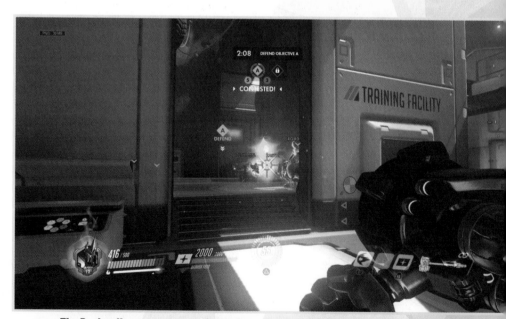

The Rocket Hammer can smack an adversary into oblivion when used at close range.

Use the Barrier Field to help team members travel safely through chokeholds and dangerous bottleneck areas. Just beware of snipers shooting from above.

Roadhog

Difficulty	Main Weapon	Ability #1	Ability #2	Ultimate Ability
*	**Scrap Gun** Depending on how it's used, this can be a short-range or mid-range weapon. Ammo spreads out after its shot.	**Chain Hook** Launch this solid metal hook and chain at your enemy, and then instantly drag him closer to you. Follow up by blasting your weapon, and you'll often complete an easier head shot.	**Take a Breather** Instantly heal yourself, and at the same time, temporarily reduce the amount of damage you receive from incoming attacks.	**Whole Hog** Knock back your enemies while continuously firing your weapon and inflicting damage.

Roadhog is a great, well-rounded Tank hero who doesn't rely on a healer.

Be sure to take advantage of Roadhog's short-range fighting capabilities
when they're needed.

The drawback to utilizing Roadhog on your team is his massive size.
He provides an easy target for your enemies. Alone, he's not good against enemies
with long-range weapons.

The Chain Hook is used to grab an enemy and quickly drag it closer.

Winston

Difficulty	Main Weapon	Ability #1	Ability #2	Ultimate Ability
**	Telsa Cannon Blast an energy beam forward that will inflict damage onto your opponents. It works well from almost any distance.	Jump Pack Jump up and land directly onto your enemy to literally flatten them. Also use this Ability to quickly jump up to higher locations within a map.	Barrier Projector Create an energy dome that will temporarily shield you and your teammates.	Primal Rage Temporarily give yourself a tremendous amount of HP. However, during this time, you can only jump and punch your enemies.

Who wouldn't want a fast-moving, genetically engineered ape on their team? He's able to climb, move quickly, and offer protection to other team members.

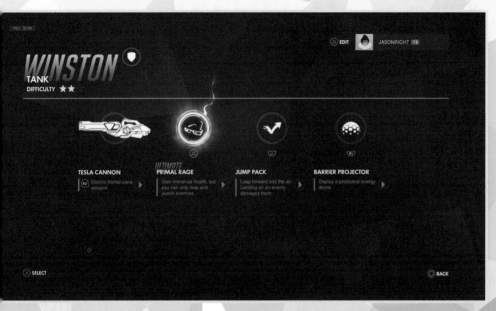

Use Winston's ability to climb to reach snipers and knock 'em off their perch.
He's great at close-range fighting.

The Telsa Cannon is Winston's primary weapon.
Use it aggressively to inflict damage on your enemies.

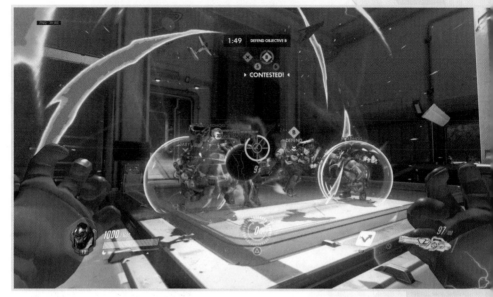

Use the Primal Rage Ultimate Ability to give yourself an energy boost during an intense battle. It's very useful when there's no Healer or Health Packs nearby.

Zarya

Difficulty	Main Weapon	Ability #1	Ability #2	Ultimate Ability
***	**Particle Cannon** Use this as a short-range energy weapon that shoots forward, or as an energy grenade launcher.	**Particle Barrier** Create a shield around yourself while inflicting harm onto your enemy.	**Projected Barrier** Create a shield around a nearby teammate to offer them protection as they launch an attack or are the recipient of an incoming attack.	**Graviton Surge** Launch a gravity weapon that wherever it lands, automatically pulls all nearby enemies towards it. This temporarily slows 'em down and groups them together for you and your teammates to then attack.

Use Zarya's Passive Energy to increase the strength of the energy shields she creates, and to increase the strength of her Particle Cannon.

Zarya's weapon makes her a very good close-range fighter. She's also very mobile.

Use Zarya in both offensive and defensive situations. She's a well-rounded Tank hero. Her Particle Cannon, however, can't land head shots, so aim toward the center of your enemies. Check out the Maximum Charge that can be unlocked from a Loot Box.

While her Projected Barrier is a useful shield, remember it doesn't last too long, so don't get caught in an open area without protection. The Graviton Surge (shown) will gather your enemies in one place, making them easy prey.

The Support Heroes

Get to know Overwatch's Support heroes. These guys are indispensable to a well-organized team.

Ana Amari

Difficulty	Main Weapon	Ability #1	Ability #2	Ultimate Ability
***	**Biotic Rifle**	**Sleep Dart**	**Biotic Grenade**	**Nano Boost**
	A long-range sniper rifle capable of harming enemies but healing allies.	This projectile weapon will put an adversary to sleep.	Throw this grenade toward allies to help heal them or use it against enemies to inflict damage and prevent them from healing.	Makes a nearby ally's weapon temporarily more powerful, while reducing the amount of damage they receive from incoming attacks.

Ana is a powerful healer who also happens to have great aim. Be sure to take advantage of both skills as they're needed. In training, practice aiming when using Sleep Darts and Biotic Grenades so these tools and weapons will become more accurate from a distance.

Remember that Ana can heal teammates from a distance,
so allies can spread out a bit as they're fighting.

If Ana gets outmuscled by an enemy, her Sleep Darts can provide a way to safely
escape. Check out this awesome skin that can be unlocked for Ana from a Loot Box.

If you're using Ana on your team, make sure stronger teammates are around to protect her. She has few HP and is unable to heal herself. She can shoot from a distance, however, to help her stay safe.

Lúcio

Difficulty	Main Weapon	Ability #1	Ability #2	Ultimate Ability
**	**Sonic Amplifier** This weapon launches a sonic projectile weapon that'll really rattle an opponent.	**Crossfade** Choose to play either of two songs in battle. One will offer a healing boost to nearby teammates, while the other will provide them with a speed boost.	**Soundwave** Use this sonic (sound-based) weapon to push enemies away.	**Sound Barrier** Create a protective shield around yourself and nearby teammates when under attack.

Use Lúcio's Amp It Up capability to increase the impact of whichever song he's playing
when using his Crossfade Ability.

Lúcio can leap onto a vertical wall, then ride along that wall
to move around a map faster.

In addition to utilizing Lúcio's healing abilities, don't forget this hero can provide teammates with a speed boost, plus offer them shielding protection during attacks. Be sure to take full advantage of all Lúcio's abilities.

Keep Lúcio moving to prevent him from becoming an easy target for your enemies. You can also use solid items in the environment to hide behind, so he stays safe.

Mercy

Difficulty	Main Weapon	Ability #1	Ability #2	Ultimate Ability
*	**Caduceus Staff** Use this tool to heal your teammates or to inflict damage on an enemy. **Caduceus Blaster** This is a versatile handheld automatic weapon.	**Guardian Angel** Fly to a teammate to reach them faster to use your healing skills.	**Resurrect** Immediately revive a teammate so they don't have to wait to respawn.	**Valkyrie** When activated, Mercy is able to fly. Plus, all her other abilities are temporarily enhanced.

Mercy's Angelic Descent ability allows her to safely leap down from high areas and slowly descend without harm. As she falls, however, she'll move forward at the same time; she does not drop straight down.

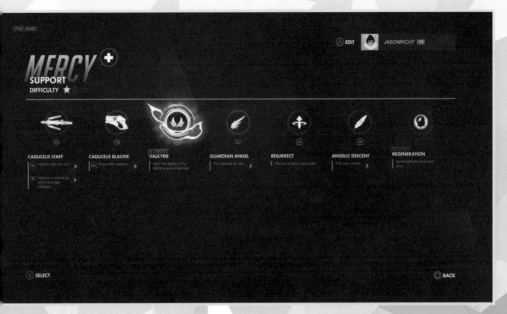

As a Support hero, Mercy will heal herself over time. You can always speed things up with a Health Pack or with the help of another Support hero.

Mercy is a much better healer than she is a fighter. While she's great at protecting team members, try to keep her from situations in which she would need to defend herself against one or more powerful enemies. When traveling in a group, keep her off the frontlines of battle.

119

Use the Caduceus Staff to heal your teammates from close- to mid-range.
From very far away, Mercy is not too useful.

Moira O'Deorain

Difficulty	Main Weapon	Ability #1	Ability #2	Ultimate Ability
**	**Biotic Grasp**	**Biotic Orb**	**Fade**	**Coalescence**
	Use biotic energy to heal the teammates in front of you. However, this can also be used as a long-range weapon that harms your enemies but simultaneously heals you and replenishes your biotic energy.	Toss this brightly colored sphere and its power will heal nearby teammates or inflict pain on nearby enemies.	When using this capability, you can't use your weapons but you can disappear from sight and move around faster without being harmed or detected.	From the palms of your hands, launch a powerful beam that will heal your teammates and seriously harm your adversaries.

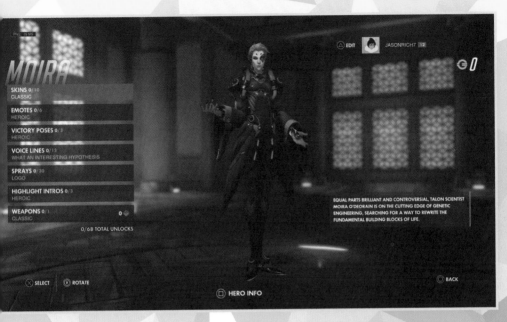

Moira can heal her allies and damage her enemies with equal finesse.

To use the Biotic Grasp as a long-range weapon requires that you keep it aimed on an enemy for an extended period for it to have its full effect. However, time isn't always on your side, and your enemy's teammates won't typically sit idle while you're attacking only one of them at a time.

Take advantage of Moira's ability to disappear, which allows her to sneak up and flank enemies from behind. Her Biotic Orb can either inflict damage to enemies, or heal teammates; it's your choice.

The Coalescence weapon can be used on multiple enemies per charge, but you need to aim it on one enemy at a time. Timing is critical when it comes to moving between enemies to get the most impact from each use.

Symmetra

Difficulty	Main Weapon	Ability #1	Ability #2	Ultimate Ability
**	**Photon Projector** Use this as a short-range weapon that inflicts more damage the longer the beam remains targeted on an enemy. The same weapon can shoot a projectile energy orb so it can alternatively be used as a long-range weapon.	**Sentry Turret** Set up this weapon, then wait for enemies to be in range before activating it. Then watch as it inflicts damage and slows down your adversaries.	**Photon Barrier** Activate an energy barrier that serves as a shield for you and your teammates. Once activated, it automatically moves forward, so stay close behind it.	**Teleporter or Shield Generator** Create a temporary teleporter that links your current location with your team's spawn room. When teammates are done respawning, they can instantly return to wherever the teleporter is set up. The Shield Generator can be used to set up a strong but stationary shield to protect yourself and your enemies.

Use the Teleporter to quickly transport teammates from the Spawn Room to your current location.

Create a temporary and stationary shield that will protect you and your teammates at the exact location you choose.

The longer you charge Symmetra's energy weapons, the more damage she inflicts. Her Photon Projector only works on one enemy at a time, however, so while she's attacking one enemy, she's potentially vulnerable to attack from others. The power is truly in her hands, as she wields no traditional weapon.

Symmetra's Teleporter can save your teammates a lot of time getting back to the battle once they've been respawned.

Zenyatta

Difficulty	Main Weapon	Ability #1	Ability #2	Ultimate Ability
***	**Orb of Destruction** Launch energy weapons from your hands in quick succession or take a moment to charge up the energy to inflict even more damage.	**Orb of Discord** Launch this even more powerful energy weapon from your hands.	**Orb of Harmony** Instantly heal your teammates by launching these special energy orbs directly at them. Zenyatta can heal her allies from a distance as long as they're visible to her.	**Transcendence** While using this temporary power, Zenyatta can't be harmed, but she can move faster and heal all her nearby teammates.

When using the Orb of Destruction, definitely aim for a head shot to achieve the most damage the fastest. Body shots are less damaging.

Zenyatta is particularly useful at healing teammates from a distance. The Transcendence move can heal multiple team members at the same time, while Zenyatta stays perfectly safe. Just be ready to get out of harm's way once the Transcendence ends.

Zenyatta is good at using one skill at a time. As a gamer, you must be able to determine when to best use each skill. First and foremost, keep your eye on your teammates and be ready to heal them as needed. When you see "Critical" icons over your teammates, this means they require urgent healing, so get to them as fast as you can.

Practice using Zenyatta as a versatile hero who can both fight and heal. Know how to use all his skills, so you can quickly adapt as different situations arise. When a lot of teammate healing needs to be done fast, take advantage of Transcendence.

Meet Overwatch's 27th Hero

In March 2018, Brigitte was added to the game as a Support hero. To learn more about this interesting new character, visit: https://playoverwatch.com/en-us/blog.

Brigitte Lindholm

Difficulty	Main Weapon	Ability #1	Ability #2	Ultimate Ability
*	**Rocket Flail** This melee weapon has a farther range than the close-range weapon of most other heroes. Swing Brigitte's right arm (while she's holding her weapon) to smash enemies.	**Repair Pack** When used on allies, Brigitte will heal her teammates. Once they're healed, continuous use increases their armor.	**Whip Shot** Use this ability to quickly push an adversary away from you.	**Rally** When activated, Brigitte can move faster, and at the same time, provide armor to teammates who are close by.

Brigitte's third ability is to create a Barrier Shield in front of her. This will protect her, and anyone standing behind her, from incoming head-on attacks.

Instead of using the Rocket Flail to harm enemies in battle,
the same maneuver will heal your allies when you strike them.

Once Brigitte's Barrier Shield (shown) is active, use the Shield Bash to quickly run
forward, stun adversaries, and knock them backwards.

SECTION X:

YOUR TRAINING HAS ONLY JUST BEGUN: OVERWATCH RESOURCES

Pro gamers around the world have created YouTube channels, online forums, and blogs focused exclusively on Overwatch. Plus, you can watch pro players compete online and describe their best strategies, or check out the coverage of Overwatch published by leading gaming websites and magazines.

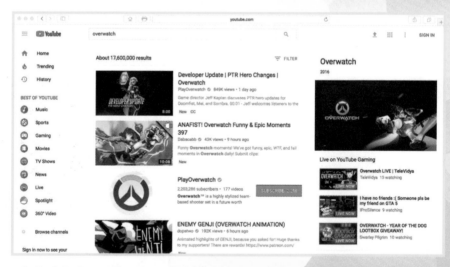

On YouTube (www.youtube.com), YouTube Gaming (https://gaming.youtube.com), or Twitch.TV (www.twitch.tv/directory/game/Overwatch), within the Search field, enter the search phrase "Overwatch" to discover many Overwatch-related channels and videos. (YouTube.com is shown here.)

Be sure to check out these awesome online resources that will help you become a better Overwatch player:

RESOURCE NAME	DESCRIPTION	URL
@PlayOverwatch	Blizzard Entertainment's official Twitter account for Overwatch.	www.twitter.com/PlayOverwatch
Blizzard Entertainment's Overwatch Website	The official website from Blizzard Entertainment that covers all things related to Overwatch.	www.playoverwatch.com
Game Informer's Overwatch Coverage	Read the latest news, articles, and reviews, plus experience all of Game Informer's coverage of Overwatch.	www.gameinformer.com/Overwatch
Gamespot's Overwatch Coverage	Read and watch all of Gamespot's coverage of Overwatch.	www.gamespot.com/overwatch
IGN Entertainment's Overwatch Coverage	Check out all IGN's past and current coverage of Overwatch.	www.ign.com/games/Overwatch
Official Overwatch Products and Gear	An online catalog offering Overwatch-themed clothing, toys, and products.	https://gear.blizzard.com/us/game/Overwatch
Overwatch Central	An independent YouTube channel originating in the UK that covers Overwatch.	www.youtube.com/channel/UCZmz0RdI6LvX_rRmrlwx0Eg
Overwatch League	The official website of the Overwatch League, in which pro gamers from around the world compete. The competitions are streamed live.	https://overwatchleague.com/en-us
Overwatch University, Reddit	An interactive message board where you can ask questions about the game, plus read text-based Q&As and discussions related to Overwatch.	www.reddit.com/r/OverwatchUniversity

(Continued on next page)

Overwatch Wiki	Produced by Gamepedia (www.gamepedia.com), this is a comprehensive and continuously updated resource that covers all aspects of Overwatch, including the latest updates and patches.	https://overwatch.gamepedia.com/Overwatch_Wiki
Play Overwatch	The official YouTube channel from Blizzard Entertainment.	www.youtube.com/channel/UCIOf1XXinvZsy4wKPAkro2A
Razer	Learn about Overwatch gaming headsets, controllers, and other PC and console peripherals, including the Razer Man o' War Tournament Edition headset.	www.razerzone.com
Turtle Beach Corp.	This is one of many companies that make awesome quality gaming headsets that work great with a PS4, Xbox One, or PC. Being able to hear crystal-clear sound and hold conversations with friends and teammates is essential when playing Overwatch.	www.turtlebeach.com
Your Overwatch	Three well-known YouTubers (Eddythechump, Weagal, and Freedo) have teamed up to create this YouTube channel that's dedicated exclusively to Overwatch.	www.youtube.com/channel/UCIOf1XXinvZsy4wKPAkro2A

The Official Overwatch Twitter Feed

Blizzard Entertainment's PlayOverwatch.com website

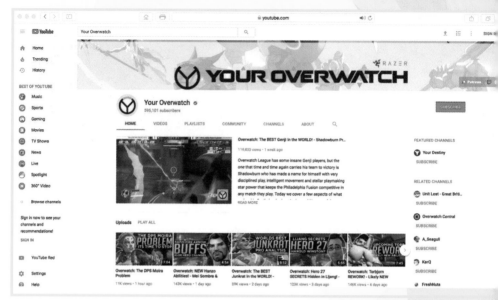

The *Your Overwatch* YouTube channel.

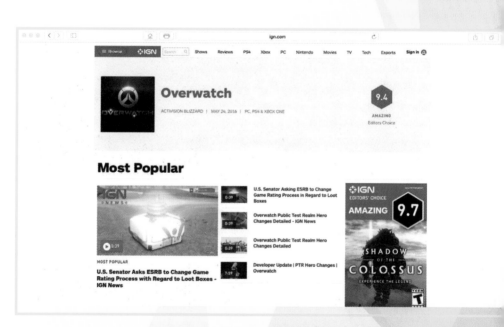

IGN's Overwatch Coverage

Check out Turtle Beach Corp.'s awesome Elite Pro gaming headset. It works well with a PS4, Xbox One, or PC. A top-quality headset is a must-have accessory for any Overwatch player.

If you're using a quality headset when playing Overwatch, you can drown out any background noise in the room and focus on sounds created by the game, such as an enemy's approaching footsteps, or enemy weapon fire coming from behind you. You can also speak directly with your team members and plan strategies in real time, as the action unfolds before your eyes.